Down River

poems by

Virginia Chase Sutton

Finishing Line Press
Georgetown, Kentucky

Down River

for Lauren

Copyright © 2017 by Virginia Chase Sutton
ISBN 978-1-63534-304-5 First Edition
All rights reserved under International and Pan-American Copyright Conventions.
No part of this book may be reproduced in any manner whatsoever without written permission from the publisher, except in the case of brief quotations embodied in critical articles and reviews.

ACKNOWLEDGMENTS

Grateful acknowledgment is made to the editors of the following publications where these poems, some of them since revised, first appeared or are forthcoming:

First published in the *Silver Birch Press My Imaginary Skill* series: The Dance Arrives at Stevenson High School
Stoneboat: Down River
Queen of Cups: Eighth Grade Graduation Ceremony; First the Argument
Amethyst Arsenic: The Menace
The Devil's Doornail, an anthology, Banshee Press: Shame
Staged reading by the Brickford Theatre and the Morris Museum, "Healing Voices On-Stage Performances," Morristown, NJ: Under the Lilacs

With deep thanks to many friends for their wisdom and support: Mark Doty, Lee Martin, Cynthia Huntington, Cynthia Hogue, Jeremy Spears, Rebecca Sutton Halonen, Constance Chase Halonen-Wilson, Constance Sutton, and Jimmy Berlin.

Publisher: Leah Maines

Editor: Christen Kincaid

Cover Art: *Cloud Study,* Johan Christian Dahl, Metropolitan Museum of Art

Author Photo: Rebecca Sutton Halonen

Cover Design: Elizabeth Maines McCleavy

Printed in the USA on acid-free paper.
Order online: www.finishinglinepress.com
　　　　　also available on amazon.com

Author inquiries and mail orders:
Finishing Line Press
P. O. Box 1626
Georgetown, Kentucky 40324
U. S. A.

Table of Contents

Gloomy Sunday 1
Down River 3
Santuario de Chimayo 5
Photo: My Grandparents' 50th Wedding
                                Anniversary Party 7
Weekend Honeymoon 9
Under the Lilacs 10
On Bipolar Depression 11
Summer Weather 13
First the Argument 15
The Menace 17
Eighth Grade Graduation Ceremony 18
The Pianos 19
Stigma 20
Shame 21
Indiana Reds 23
The Dance Arrives at Stevenson High School 24
Study Group 26
On the Road to California 27
Vacation Bible School 29
The Kill Me Pills 30
Handbag 32
Discarded Tears 33
After Midnight at the Psych Hospital 34

Gloomy Sunday

is any evening when Mother listens to Billie Holiday
on full blast, the song playing on repeat. She's suffering.
Mother's suffering. Billie's voice slips up the stairs,
liquid heartbreak as she sings *My heart is telling you/
How much I wanted you.* And I feel my bones

shudder. When the pills no longer work, when
the booze has lost its magic, Mother must be arguing
with her own demons, something she believes
no one understands. And as the song twirls on the turntable,
there will be trouble ahead. Lady Day's despair fills

the house: *Death is no dream.* I'm twelve, know something
about loss and the depth of sorrow from illicit touching
and kisses from my father when he climbs beneath my covers,
after roaming the house. Finally finding me, taking me. I'm his
own. But he travels every other week, a salesman, leaves me

alone with Mother. Most nights I try to sleep beneath the layer
of smoke, high school boy chatter, and the stereo though she
never plays Billie for them. This is her end-of-the-line song,
bitterness and regret for her marriage, for being stuck with children,
for the way her life of teaching is never enough, and how she must feel

all that pain down deep in her heart, should she have one. How many
secrets must Mother have? Even boozed-up, staggering from too many
pills and so much alcohol, Mother never tells though she climbs
the stairs, her gait both heavy and measured—*With the last breath
of my soul,/ I'll be blessin' you.* A suicide song that sends Mother

in search of a reason to stay alive. I hear her heading for me. I've
been reading, doing a school project on utopian life, loving each
book I've read, relishing the perfection of their glorious lives,
no matter how short-lived the colony. Most of the time
I just read for me, as far into the night as I can get away with.

But tonight I snap off the light. Then my bedroom door slams open
and her shadow cast from the hall light is enormous though she's
of ordinary size. I clearly hear *Angels have no thought/ Of ever
returning you./Would they be angry/If I thought of joining you?*
With great strength, she pulls me out of bed and I stand before her

1

on the cold hardwood floor, shivering from weather and for what
I know comes next. I can barely see that her baby blue
tent dress is spattered with drops and splotches of bourbon.
Did this happen when she couldn't reach her mouth, I think
to myself. She spews a list of complaints about me—

I'm too fat, too homely to be the child of a beauty such
as she, I'm doing poorly in school though my IQ shows
I should be acing all my work. O, the list seems endless:
Let them not weep, let them know that I am glad to go Billie

croons, unmistakably forlorn. Verbal barbs continue
but I refuse to cry, which pisses Mother off even further.
Finally she does what I hate most: she sidles up close,
grips my chin with a fist made of metal. I can see her bleary
hazel eyes, smell the fetid odor of too many cigarettes and

too many drinks. Her bloated once-beautiful face stares at mine,
inches away. She says *I love you so much it hurts saying I love you.*
This abstract idea, certainly never mentioned except on *Gloomy Sunday*
nights, is so false it burns my skin. With a flourish, Mother shoves me
towards bed. Done with me, she leaves—*With shadows I spend it all.*

O Mother, o weeping Mother: *Sunday is gloomy,/ My hours are slumberless./
Dearest the shadows/ I live with are numberless.* Early in the morning,
before school, I'll find Mother passed out someplace in the house
in her own piss. Though this place is small, she could have collapsed
anywhere, and eventually will. Billie Holiday's still on repeat on the turntable

Down River

Jouncing in the rear of our neighbor's powerboat,
I'm certain I'll fall into the murky waters
of the Mississippi River. A sunlit morning. Splashing
water drifts over me like rain until we reach the sandbar.

I stagger onto a squishy surface. My parents and Mr. and Mrs. Vogel
drink beer while we four kids—two of us and their two boys—
explore the span but we are nowhere. We have a picnic
of peanut butter and jelly sandwiches, filch chips from the neighbors

when Mother isn't looking. Mr. Vogel and my father
get back into the boat, head for a pier-side grocery for more
beer. We sizzle in the sun. I'm an over-ripe tomato from
the acre Mother planted behind the house. *Come on* Mother shouts

suddenly to Mrs. Vogel. *We're going to have some fun.* They drag
inner tubes to water's edge, climb into the centers, drift away.
Mother's drunk. Both sets of parents have abandoned us. Surrounding
us the area is dangerous with deep drop-offs and uncertain currents

though I don't think about it until our mothers disappear, their
bright hair twinkling on the wavy water, and they are long gone.
There is nothing to do but build castles out of muddy sand.
My sister and I work against the boys. They have plenty of practice,

easily beat us with turrets and a moat. *We come here every
weekend* Steve explains. *But my mother never left before.* I blush,
shamed, but my face is too red to tell. I look at our sandcastle
and it is a tumble-down mess, much like our house. At last

we hear the boat in the distance as it smacks the water, then *putt-putts*
toward the sandbar. *Where the hell are your mothers* my father bellows.
They bobbed and floated on the water, then vanished I say. We are
brilliant and lovely in summer's sun, though six-year-old Dave is trying

not to cry. The fathers push off, following the women. Briefly,
our younger siblings sniffle with abandon, and Steve and I embrace them.
The sun, always uncertain in St. Louis, drifts behind clouds heavy with rain.
It's suddenly semi-dark. Lightning etches the sky. We don't know

danger—four forgotten children on a shifting sandbar, currents gulping
mud and muck. We watch thrilling flashes across darkness. I know the boys
are thinking of their mother. It seems forever before the four adults return.
Mother and Mrs. Vogel floated pretty far downstream, laughing in their

drunkenness. We heard their voices on echoing wind as we sat on
dirty sand, watching their magic. But when they return, there is nothing
but silence. Remains of our picnic, hours ago, are packed up
and we fall into the powerboat. Reversing slowly from the sandbar

as it crumbles, nibbled by waves, we go fast after we drift into deeper water.
Not a word is spoken. The beer my father and Mr. Vogel purchased sits
on the cooler. Even Mother's smart enough not to reach for one,
though I know she wants to. Back at the boat launch at last, we clamber

into our station wagon while my father helps Mr. Vogel get the boat
onto its trailer. We leave with a small *thank you* to the family—
they don't notice. At home, my parents have a terrific fight, mostly
about Mother's drinking, but also over my father's deeply welled anger

concerning the safety of four young children alone on collapsing
sand. He doesn't mention that he left us to chase the women.
There's a lot of swearing and a number of threats, mostly
from my father who yells *I'm really leaving this time* though

it's emptiness. Mother pours a drink from the bottle she keeps
in a kitchen cabinet, ignoring him. The next day, Steve and Dave come
to our house to play outside. They have to straddle the broken-down
swing set in the backyard as our big mean dog leaps into air, trying

to bite their feet. They wear black high-top tennis shoes, something
the dog hates. We call ourselves boyfriends and girlfriends, at least
for now, somehow certain our parents will not be friends anymore and
the boys will not be allowed over to our house to play. My sister and I

never go on an outing again in the big powerboat, never eat on
a sandbar in the mighty river, terrified, as we watch, minute
by minute, mud diminishing, filthy water seeping towards
our nearly naked bodies, our icy shriveled toes.

Santuario de Chimayo

By chance, we arrive at this small adobe church
while touring wineries between Santa Fe and Taos.
It's a healing place for pain, illness, and disabilities.
Late in the afternoon, crowds gone, we're the only
pilgrims here. Workers box up used tall candles. I

go to the store up the hill to purchase a couple, and
it's closed. Desolate for some reason, I sit on one
of the wooden benches facing the chapel and a worker,
feeling sorry for me, offers two candles, already used
by someone else in prayer. One is marked with Jesus

and the other Our Lady of Guadalupe. My husband and I
enter into the suddenly cool church, marvel at artwork.
Founded on private land in 1816 it is now a National
Historic Landmark compared by most to Lourdes. It
attracts more than 300,000 pilgrims a year. Right now,

the place holds only we two. I light the candles at
the altar, one for each of my parents as I always do
at any Catholic church I might wander into. Non-believer,
I cannot explain this action—after years of sexual abuse
from my father and taunts and meanness from my mother

I'm glad both are dead. In a small room to the right, a
pit holds soft dirt and a trowel so those who do believe
may fill containers with the holy dirt, scraped from
the hills of the *Sangre de Cristo* mountains. Deeply
inhaling, I'm certain dust has gone into my lungs,

offering protection. Rapidly approaching a huge mental
breakdown, I could use some help. To the left is a prayer
room filled with discarded crutches, walkers, and wheelchairs.
Smiling photos of the cured plaster the walls and white messages
paper the room in layers—*heal my son, help my father's heart grow*

strong, let my baby live. Plea after plea for divine intervention.
As we leave, the chapel's locked behind us. Dimly I know
I'm unwell, but never even thought to leave a note behind.
This has been a trip simply to sample and purchase wine;
we had no knowledge of this place or the pilgrimage made

each year during Holy Week by believers who walk thirty miles from Santa Fe to the shrine. We happen upon it by accident or some sort of miracle. Off we go to visit one more winery. We drive past dusty clusters of grapes hanging from vines cascading down wooden arbors, jeweled arches we walk through.

Photo: My Grandparents' 50th Wedding Anniversary Party

I'm the girl at the end of the line of cousins, dressed in a navy blue
old-lady fat suit two sizes too big, purchased from the Montgomery Ward
catalogue. My sister joins our first cousins, all dressed alike in mini skirts,

their long hair parted neatly down the middle. They smile prettily, certain
of their loveliness. We are so young. At the request of some distant cousin
shooting the photo, they raise their right legs and hike up their skirts, as if

aiming for a high kick. Knees up, they practically skim their own chins.
Their smiles, deep and open, white teeth grinning, heads tossed back as if
to claim their own sexuality. I've been herded as anchor, belonging

because my sister's here, because we six are the only grandchildren. I'm
one of them, but not really, wearing a half-grin of embarrassment, a red scarf
tied around my neck, which is the color of my face, though this photo's

black and white. I do as I'm told. I grip the left shoulder of my youngest
cousin, do not, could not raise my leg with such abandon. A stranger inside
this outfit, inside my skin. Everyone at the party takes note of me, so

inappropriately dressed. Some stare in kindness, most in pity for the young
teenager attired in a pantsuit her own grandmother would reject as too old,
too ugly, too wrong for life. *The scarf* says the catalogue *draws the eye*

up from the body, frames the face. Designed to be slimming, it's awkward
instead. It isn't working for me. I'm holding down the line of beauty—my
round face looks away from joy, off to the right side, away from the girls.

How sad I don't know what to wear, how to choose clothing from a catalogue,
my go-to for attire, instead of a dress shop for this momentous, happy
occasion. Sure, I'd never be able to wear a skirt that I might flip up,

a gesture unknown to me, so unfamiliar, but I know I could look better,
not this big blue whale surfacing. Adorable, these granddaughters beside
me. I'm the fool in the polyester nightmare. I know this lecherous

cousin taking the photo, someone I have never met before, wants me out.
The soft summer air drifts over us and it smells like sex. Somehow
the others have inhaled this scent drifting through the grove of apple

trees behind the house. *Shame on you* I want to say to this distant man, exploiting teenage girls in their still innocence. But I'm too afraid to speak, pulled into the photo when he must wish me out. I cannot talk

about any of the wrongs of my life, my mother's disinterest and meanness, my father who still climbs in and out of my bed as he has for years, my sister's inattention and lucky life outside our house that she has discovered

for herself. But by god I plaster a smile, let the breeze pass me by, trapped in an uncomfortable outfit, wishing I could sneak away, unwanted and painfully dressed, and let that sweet, tangy odor hit me hard.

Weekend Honeymoon

After three quick weeks, my parents just knew. It was
married love they pined for. Still strangers who
forgot about college, spending all their time
in the sack. They had met one afternoon on the quad,
practically running into one another, both late to class.

She was eighteen, just out of high school with auburn hair
she could sit on. He was twenty-one, back from the Army Air Corps,
urged into education by his older sister. One afternoon, dressed
in her gray graduation suit, her hair flowed against her pale skin
and he, darkly handsome, was in his only suit. It was black. On

a Thursday morning, skipping school, they drove from Indiana
to Kentucky to be married. One stop for a corsage, her wedding flowers.
They stopped at the first justice-of-the peace where she lied, claimed
she was twenty-one. Decades later, after complaining about their
marriage, he told me *it was never love, just a sexual thing.* But in

that moment, they posed for a wedding portrait beneath a trellis
of artificial camellias. She smiled, dimples flashing, eyes looking
away from the camera while he faced it, dead on, shell-shocked
and clumsy. His tie was crooked. They checked-in early next door
at the *Bide-a-Wee Motel*. They vibrated with love and the urge

for constant touch. They spent their time having married sex,
something they liked quite a bit. The next day they drove back,
anxious for married student housing. Permission granted, they shared
a Quonset Hut divided into three tiny apartments. They decorated
with cast-off things from his parents. Had loud sex in both rooms.

On the kitchen table, on the counter, on the stained mattress on the floor.
They didn't care but smoked cigarettes after every act, just like in
the movies. She, a beauty, with hazel eyes she kept open every minute.
His eyes were brown, his skin dark from working in the greenhouse
and playing baseball with his hometown buddies. On Monday, grinning,

my parents went back to summer school. Thin gold bands adorned their
fingers. They gleamed, they glittered. How they proudly displayed
themselves after a three-day honeymoon. How the other students admired
them, their happiness radiating, so jealous that the two of them were
off the market for good, playing house down the hill, behind the college.

Under the Lilacs

Fragrantly looming bushes in the front yard
face the street, thickets with secrets. It's where

I hide all spring and summer. I'm far away
from my mother's cigarettes clenched between

her lips, spewing smoke and commands. It all drifts
through the screen door, into my garment of leaves.

Sometimes rain drips onto dusty greenery, bending
spiked flowers, their sweetness cascading

my small room. Mostly, birds bicker above me, small nests
made from my hair and twigs. I'm safe here,

enchanted. Neighborhood kids move back and forth
on the sidewalk, a short distance away, but they don't

miss me. I watch from my cave at their pleasure
together, embraced by overgrown branches.

Wind blows blue and lavender blooms, growing
inside out. Tidbits falling, swaying far above.

I'm flat on hard-packed earth, tucking myself in
each morning, out only for a bologna sandwich at noon.

Leaves rattle me to sleep, knit me into place.
Invisible, I wait. Hiding where I might die

this afternoon, amidst perfume and bird noise,
and all of those who have forgotten me.

On Bipolar Depression

You can feel water pulling away, heading out
to sea leaving behind junk on the sand—soda cans,
flopping fish, even dull bits of beach glass. You
have a collection in a bowl in your study, love
to feel this almost-pinch as you circle one with

your worried left hand. That dark water matches
the depression, down deep in your brain, place
where you try not to wander. *This is only temporary*
you say aloud. *These feelings will pass* and try to go about
your life, small though it is. Every time echoes of despair

try to smother, you must whisper *this is not real*. You avoid
going back to bed when it is all you can do. You see the lucky
striped blanket, the one you have taken to every
psych hospitalization. It reminds you of home,
that living is okay. You are clever at the hospital,

how you hide your pen in your journal, slip it between
the pillow case and your head to make it disappear—nurses'
aides who wanted to take them for contraband, even with
a doc's special order. They never found them. You carried
the book and pen to the nurses' station, waved it in triumph,

a sign you weren't better. But now the bed beckons with each
faded strip of pink, purple, green, yellow. It knows who you are.
But you refuse to return to an embrace, memories of safety fading.
I feel waves of despair wash over me you tell your new therapist,
hardly an original phrase. But you are in too deep to think of something

poetic, maybe something profound. *What are you doing about this
depression* your new therapist asks and you repeat what is engraved
in your head: *this feeling is only temporary* and *I refuse to go back
to bed*. O, these are the correct things as he nods. *Good, good* he says,
nodding. *Keep on doing that*. You do not tell him you are choking

on sea water even though you are at least six hours from LA,
too far from your desert home to suffocate. You do not tell him
you rise before dawn, listen to birds chatter in the back yard.
In the distance, you hear a buzz of birdsong but only one lonely bird
is in your yard, shorn of trees. It's pointless to tell your new therapist

about your old therapist, who died of surgical complications this time
in spring two years ago. How you wave as you pass the cemetery
on your way to your new therapist's office. Seven years ticked by
in a moment, the time you spent with him, rich and honest. You speak
to him as you drive past, know he's listening, that he hears your despair.

Standing on the tile in the kitchen, both hands clutching ice cubes.
Cold water drips down your outstretched arms. *I'm in the here
and now* you say, shivering. *I'm in the here and now.* It's a trick
you learned from your dead therapist. How you cry, mixture
of hot and cold, tears rivulets down your puffy cheeks. You

keep scooping ice, trying to make your brain flip over. *I'm
in the here and now* you repeat. Somehow you keep saying it,
as if you believe it, in a puddle of water. But it's
the nature of things—that ice melts quickly in the kitchen's
warm air, your brain frozen into sections, good and bad. That

beach glass is tossed to water's edge, that waves and wavelets
head out to sea, and that you dream of beaches you have known.
And your notebook is fallow and you finally give in, wrap
the blanket around your body and sit in your bed, thinking
darkness, dreaming darkness, becoming darkness.

Summer Weather

Late afternoon in the basement, scent of coal dust
and suds from Gramma's washing machine stop up
my nose. Grampa has a transistor radio blaring weather
reports. An hour ago he came inside, telling us *I don't
like that sky.* My sister and I—snapping beans at the table—
are also Midwesterners, know exactly what that means:

tornado. He wiped his work boots at the door, hurried to
the TV set on the edge of the crimson rug Gramma vacuums
every morning. We followed, ducking to peek out the windows.
A looming black sky. The TV sang a high tune, cautioning
rural residents to take cover. Gramma ushered us down,
calling *hurry, Millard* over her shoulder. Now in the belly

of the house, sitting side-by-side, my sister and I clutch hands.
Grampa joins us, says *no twister yet.* We see leaves stripped
from the apple orchard whip past tiny basement
windows. Electricity flickers and the bulb hanging from
the ceiling on a long cloth cord sputters out. From time to
time, Grampa turns on the radio as the storm moves past.

We hear the all-clear signal, make our way upstairs in the dark
for a cold supper of peanut butter on *Ritz Crackers* and *Coke*
in tall glasses. Gramma leads us upstairs to bed with a candle
and we agree to share a bed instead of sleeping each in her
own room. We hear the steady thrum of rain on the roof and
sudden gusts of wind. In the morning, we clean up the yard,

gather all the lost green apples that blew off trees. One tree
is split in half and a neighbor's clothes line is wrapped around
another, clothes still pinned on. *We'll go see the destruction* Gramma
calls and bundles us into the huge blue car. Traveling back country
roads we pass houses and barns without roofs. Big trees are
uprooted, snaky roots clogged with mud. We stop when a cop

flags us down. A huge fallen tree stretches across the road.
*Folks, another storm's about to blow through. You better get
along home.* Grampa rotates the car as it begins to pour.
Windshield wipers madly click as he hurries us home. We pass
through a small town where a tornado siren howls. My sister
and I are allies again, holding hands on the hard plank seat.

Once home, it's back to the basement, the car left in the gravel
driveway. Grampa's warning the tenants in the two apartments
in the big house and we hear them stumble down the stairs on the other
side of the basement. It seems like forever. Wind whips the windows
and it feels like a train's rushing through. The dangling light snuffs
so we sit in the dark, rain torrential against the panes.

First the Argument

This breezy, early summer afternoon, doors and windows
glued shut. Downstairs upraised voices are escalating. Familiar
fights my sister and I hear when our father is home on
weekends. We hide halfway up the living room stairs,
risky spot where we might get caught. *Mary Ellen, dammit,*

you are drunk he bellows, disgust curdling his
thick voice. She has been drinking steadily today,
since mid-morning. A few quiet beers, now martinis, until
evening when she will switch to bourbon, always trouble.
We gauge her drunkenness from a distance. Not a ten, like

nearly every evening now. But when our father is home
it's a controlled seven. Drinking early on a Saturday is bad news,
asking for trouble, asking for our father's unwanted attention.
We strain to hear. Mother's crying, something rare, but
becoming more frequent. My sister and I exchange looks—

jaws unhinged, panic in our eyes. Suddenly the *splat* of flesh
hitting the kitchen's dirty linoleum, angry shrieks of fear—
too many emotions to name. We stand, pad down the stairs,
see our father standing over Mother, clenching his fat
hands. Skirt hiked, blue varicose veins splotches of color

on her white legs, she sees us. *He hit me, he hit me.* Cagey
like our dog licking our dinner plates when Mother's head
is turned, our father says *I did not* while squeezing his fists.
Get up off the floor he orders but she cannot stand. Tangled
in her blue tent dress wrapped around her waist, she is unable

to coordinate. Finally she rolls on her belly, kneels, clutches
the stovetop, pulls herself to her feet. We stare as she wavers
from one foot to another. I see a bright pink mark on her left cheek
shaped like a palm print. *He pushed me* she wails. The frightened dog
moves to stand behind us as we block the entrance into the kitchen

from the dining room. Our father turns his back, but first
I glimpse a sneer across his handsome face. My sister and I
are accustomed to Mother's drunken behavior but how careless
has she been to get this drunk on a weekend? Is this scene
the beginning of something even more terrible? The house

is stifling and I want to give her a pass for today but
it's no-go. She's a nine—I have miscalculated—her pretty face
smeared with snot and tears. It's early yet, the sun shining,
lilac bushes outside bending in the breeze, not breaking,
nowhere near sweeping the grass, nowhere near the floor.

The Menace

Trapped in late nighttime's vapor, pale
white threads like smoke from my parents'
constantly lit cigarettes, it sneaks into

the house beneath a window sill. It brings
a fetid odor heavier than air as it sinks
to the floor of my bedroom, fills the space

beneath my bed where it lingers, hoping
for an errant limb that might travel to
the edge of covers, where my careless body

might spill. It coils in the closet, rubbing
against garments, already ghostly on their
hangers, working its way from neckline

to hem, then slips between layers of cloth.
On to the next dress, leaving nothing untouched.
I know it very young. It follows me from

earliest childhood. Sometimes I see it in
the dark, silver apparition, outlines like a man,
big as my father, fine as dust. We move

from house to house, state to state, leave the
menace. For a night or two, I might say *it's
gone* but soon enough, it sweeps into

my room through cracks in the walls. As an
adult, it fades, yet follows me from college
to college, slithers beneath my marriage bed.

And inside depression's black lake, it haunts,
willing to grab at anything. And in several
psych hospitals, humming at bedtime, it stumbles

after me, hiding beneath my bed. Still a puff
of smoke, it loves me into daylight where
I can finally dismount the bed, step into slippers,

safe as I move along my day's journey.
Dust and shadows await me as it watches,
ready to work itself into my night.

Eighth Grade Graduation Ceremony

A commotion splits heavy silence at the back of the gym
and I suspect the woman singing, laughing, finally swearing
is my mother, hustled out, drunk and stupid. Most of the audience
has turned in their seats to witness and it is only when the slam
of heavy doors echoes that they turn again as Principal Teeter
calls the next name and the ceremony continues. Up on stage,

near the back row, my face is as red as it gets every summer
when my sister and I are sent to the town's swimming pool
beneath a Midwestern yellow yolk sun. Carefully I pick up
the gold charm in the shape of a piece of fancy Valentine candy
hanging from a long necklace and press it to my ear. I hear
a faint whir and I breathe slowly in and out with each movement.

It nestles in the center of the lace jabot, only decoration on my
flour sack dress. I'm forced to wear this because it was the only
one in white in my size and I look dreadful—my fat arms hang,
my white pumps pinch, my stockings hooked to my panty girdle
barely fit. For once, my parents have gotten it right. Girls
have been wearing candy watches all year. *So much sexier*

than wristwatches I think. Tonight is the conclusion of middle school,
no great achievement, I believe, but others do, plan parties and
celebrations to which I'm not invited. My father has promised
to buy ice cream from *Walgreens* but I'm sure that will not happen
now. I know this just as I'm certain my mother was the woman
dragged out of the ceremony, much to everyone's shock. After all

is done, I wait on the curb for my father to pick me up. He flips open
the passenger door. *Sorry kid* he says. *It took three guys and me
to carry your mother to the car where she passed out.* He snaps
his lighter, inhales his cigarette. The watch is ticking against my chest
and I feel my heart explode. *I will visit you late tonight* he says, his
face smooth as it glows from the dashboard. My father's hand expertly

settles on my silky left knee. *I love you* he says as we drive away.
Tick-tock, tick-tock—how many hours to pleasure, to pain? Finally
he nestles beside me in my basement bedroom where the candy watch
sits squarely on my pink dressing table. I hear it above my own breath.
Let us forget my father says, touching me like an expert. I stare at
peeling cowboy wallpaper across the room, merely a minor distraction.

The Pianos

Mother's a gifted pianist, so my father says, with a decade
of lessons at a baby grand. But she will not play since their
marriage. Now she hates such music. Waxing her abilities,
my father says her long fingers were once smoothly easy over

ivory keys. My father sight-reads music, plays honky-tonk
on his mother's ebony upright every time we visit far-away Indiana.
Stop it, Bob Mother mutters near his ear, tugging at the orange belt
circling her waist. *Just stop right now.* He turns on the piano stool,

handsome face melting beneath the bright sun of her blue and orange
dotted dress. At home we briefly have a piano rented by the month
though Mother goes outside to chain smoke during lessons. My parents
want my sister and I to learn, tatters from Mother's now despised

and privileged childhood. Neither of us is talented. Tin-eared,
I stumble through instruction books. I can locate middle C,
the rest of the long black and white keys all the same, seemingly
equally far away to my seven-year-old hands. I'm forced to practice

every day. My little sister picks it up faster but she is not very good either.
Years later—the rental returned, house and business lost, a move
to another state—we are a home without an instrument. Then my parents'
milkman friend gifts us with an old upright with a broken sound board

one of his wealthy customers wants to give away. Frightfully out of tune,
it has a Victorian stool with curves and curlicues. In a decade my father
will break the stool when he throws it at my sister after she misses curfew,
shattering it to bits. But for now he loves to play, lives to play, but

Mother does not allow it. Following her brain aneurysm, she is meaner,
cursing him if he goes near the instrument. If he attempts a few bars
of a Christmas carol, Mother screams her hatred—at him, at the piano,
at joy. He only plays when she's at the beauty salon every Saturday.

I confess I tire of forties hits and honky-tonk. But I understand his heart
is a beat-up thing. The piano takes up an entire living room wall. I want him
to play, I want his body to soar with his limited gift, nothing like Mother's
though I never hear her strike a note or see her stroke the keys.

Stigma

You slump in your car after your therapy session is over, thinking *how much longer can I go on?* Behind the fence and down the steep hill, golfers roam the plush course, their cheers and laughter wafting through your open window. Tired of labels—bipolar, major depression, PTSD—things *tick-tocking* inside your head that cost your job, your profession, finances, friends. Those who could not bear the manic you, baking and decorating dozens of Valentine cookies for your best friend, too-frantic conversations, or those who hate your darkness, saturation of minute moments, curving them into webs. Sure, you know you are broken, lack the razzle-dazzle of the old days, pre-diagnosis, pre-medication. Now you count friends on one hand, not even enough to form a palm to shoo the old life away, good-bye, driving streets toward home.

Shame

After one dreadful sexual experience,
both of us unsatisfied, after you shove
into my snatch, me wanting you out,
you calm on a tip of the quarter moon.

We agree to be just friends, never lovers again,
swearing on that beam of light. A couple
of weeks later, I go dancing with you, something
we are good at, our feet kicking magical moon

drops falling from the disco ball rotating overhead.
This is something two friends would do. But
I drink too much, tossing back gin and tonics
you feed me, dizzy and dull as rain. Glass after

glass. I blackout. At dawn, I stagger awake,
and you are naked beside me. I stare at a parade
of seven used condoms neatly lining the dresser.
I rise, wrap the sheet around my achy body

and puke. It all spills out—booze, you, the sex
I don't remember. You are still in my bed
when I return, laughing smugly. *You were quiet
for the first time in your life* you say smoothly,

your perfect body too close. Once I admired
your muscles, the way your flesh shifted
as you moved. *No* I say and you laugh. What
kind of man pushes hard into my center,

manipulates my body while I'm unconscious?
Time to go you say, dress in an instant, your brown
leather jacket gleaming as you slither out the front door.
I blame myself for my drunkenness, the unknowing

of last night and now new day during an immediate
hot shower, tears and snot running down my face
until only cold water remains. I try to scrub you
away, the sun rising outside though I hide

from it, from friends. I say *too much drinking, too
much dancing in the circle of his arms.* But I'm
only guessing. I was passed out cold. A lesson
in self-loathing, my wet hair tucked behind

my ears so I might hear if you dared return. But you
don't, your revenge slaked. Years later a student
in my composition class gives an oral report on
date rape. As she talks, I'm suddenly short

of breath, trembling, recalling your fingerprint
bruises on my body, the way the day rose,
as if it were any other day, as if nothing had
happened. Sick in my gut, shaking,

I abruptly dismiss the class, flip off the cruel
overhead light, place one burning
cheek against a cool desktop in the back
of the room. I see you, flames fanning

behind you, lighting the room, you
pointing again to used condoms,
so amused at my disbelief. They were
trophies, though I don't understand

why. Please call me something beautiful
to take back that night and morning—lily,
flower. But for you I am an unwilling vessel,
your handsome cock wrapped snugly in

my gorgeous vagina. Because of you
I learn never to trust the moon's
bright gleam. How I remember vomiting
again and again, not knowing, years

of humiliation and shame ahead. Me
blaming me, violated in the most
basic of ugly ways. How you dare
to take me, curtains open, bed inviting,

me a lumpy sack, eyes glued shut. I woke
to your amusement and deep happiness.
Stop and take a breath. Turn my head
on the desk in the room where I have

control, responsibility. I now know what
you did, despite my best intentions.
Today outside the empty classroom,
I know the sun beats and steams.

Indiana Reds

Spongy grass nestles my body until I flatten it. Above me, a white and blue striped sky, small airplane puttering along. Then it smoothly releases a rope and the tag-along glider lifts on a breeze. In the small orchard behind my grandparents' roomy house, small red wounds hover in shiny leaves. My sister calls, up high on a ladder, tossing bloody fruit into a basket down below. She pitches a couple towards me. They plop. Is her aim off or is her pitching arm sore? Between swaying branches, I see a silver plane and glinting glider. They float not far from the small airport down the narrow highway running in front of my grandparents' house, the first Baptist church in the county. If we gather enough of the delicious fruit Gramma will make pie for supper, a treat we will eat off trays in front of the TV, something never allowed at home. *Catch it this time* my sister directs as I stand beneath the tree. The apples, the apples, a sloppy mess in the basket. I inspect them, discard the bruised, the wormy, searching for perfection. There will be enough for two pies as yet another plane croons above us and I imagine the uncoupling of a glider. How it cruises clouds, then finds its way back to the airport, narrow runway, the earth.

The Dance Arrives at Stevenson High School

My feet flash across the stage. I act twenty-one
loving the *tap-tap-tap-tap* as in my head I
automatically repeat *shuffle-ball-change,*

shuffle-ball-change. I'm dressed like a Vegas
showgirl—a sequined and feathered headdress
pinned into my upswept brown hair. My right hand

brushes the right shoulder of the girl ahead of me
as we dance. And our costume is spectacular!
A one-piece bathing-suit style, shimmering white

fabric layered in shivering black sequins, the
bosom encrusted with crystals. The entire back
is black with bands of sparkle. O, how I shine.

In full-dress make-up, my rouged lips and cheeks
are o-so-kissable. And my eyes with jeweled lashes
are visible even to the last row of the auditorium.

On my feet, classic black patent leather tap shoes
tied up with black ribbon. Underneath are silver
taps making the impossible possible. We slowly

move from stage left to stage right in a straight
line, three girls ahead of me and seventeen
behind. The row heads behind heavy red velvet

curtains, music blaring, taps amplified. So practiced
are we that it's just a moment before we turn in unison,
head back out. Then we pause, *tap-tap* our way towards

the audience. We're doing the Rockettes proud. As one,
we bow, link arms and high kick as our big finish,
legs bending, thrust out, bending, repeating our way

into near breathlessness. We gleam, we are glory.
Unflappable we turn and leave the way we arrive,
the girl behind me skimming my translucent skin. Our

costumes are bright bites of breathtaking dazzle as we dissolve
into the wings. Curtains swish shut and applause roars. Opening
again, we each gracefully hold a sheaf of multi-colored roses.

We bow right, left, center. The crowd whistles, jumps to
their feet. I'm collecting admirers, I know it, in this deluge
of sweetness, sparking rhinestones, the heat of heavy tap shoes

Study Group

On school nights, Monday through Thursday, while
my father is on the road, the boys come over. They arrive
early evenings, just after my sister and I have finished

choking down still-frozen TV dinners. Mother is high
on martinis, before the despair when she clicks open
the bourbon bottle. Each night is different but my sister

and I are smart enough to scuttle upstairs, hide in our rooms.
They are Mother's high school students, years older than
we are. Some nights are rowdy as Mother feeds them martinis,

very dry, carrying a pitcher to serve them, cigarette balanced
between her lips. The guys fetch glasses from the kitchen
even washing those in the sink. Other nights are quieter, tangy

scent in the air, mellow music drifting on the stereo, LPs
scattered across the rug. They snack on treats bought at
the convenience store since they know our cupboards are bare,

holding only *Diet Rite* soda and cans of *Metracal*. Smoking
pot, they hunker on the rug where Mother sits while grading
English papers. When it is too loud or too quiet, I sneak

halfway downstairs, hidden by a wall though I can hear and smell
everything. I never creep where I might be seen—I just want
to peek. Smoke from six or seven cigarettes curls its way up

the stairs. The entire house is shaded blue. It gets late.
A couple of boys stagger out the front door, the rest of the group
laughing uproariously at nothing. Once in a while, Mother

takes a lover, but only if she has switched to bourbon, the gin buzz
not working. She unzips her yellow housedress, strips, splays
open her legs to him—whoever he may be—and they have at it

in the semi-dark room. Even though it is past midnight, I haven't
slept, cannot sleep in this bruised house. Sometimes my sister
joins me in observation but she can sleep, stay asleep, even

as the boys leave. The roar of their revved up cars echoes
on our quiet suburban street, just down the road from school.
Finally they head home, wherever that is, whatever they must be.

On the Road to California

Jaunting to Disneyland, car jammed
with suitcases, a baby. I remember
my last trip west. Forced into a psychiatric hospital,

locked in a box for thirty-one days. Soft bruises
of sky, a quiet chill. I stumble through mattresses
dragged down the hall by ghosts, patients

asleep on the floor by the nurses' station
to avoid self-harm—no ink pens to the wrist,
or staples as weapons torn from a self-help

magazine. Bipolar, ashamed, language
musical only to myself, watching personalities
flash across the faces and bodies of other patients.

I lose time myself with a lick of DID, robo-walk
through days of group therapy. *You are not
a boulder, a rock without feeling* my hospital therapist

says, deep into our first meeting. Tears whisk
corners of my eyes, ocean pounding blocks away.
My father stalks me here, long-ago dead

but living now in corners, wants to shush me
with his mouth, broken skin across his knuckles,
bloating blood. It's so difficult to speak up.

He creeps in camouflage, crumpled
pajamas, back to childhood's bed when
the whole house hushes. Ignoring my *yes* or *no*.

Safe in this small hospital, where crisis blooms.
He draws near. Patients know him,
and are afraid. I shiver in California's sweet

November. Today it is February in Disneyland,
Throngs of shoving people. The baby cries. Easy
to recall the hospital, long for salty safety again.

March into trauma group, listen to women
scream. I'm no different. I long for my mind
to be clean as a coastal breeze. Lovely silence

as aides snap a flashlight in my face, every fifteen
minutes for weeks. I'm a dutiful woman now,
though he still comes to me. Finally, I drag

my suitcase, lavender-scented kerchief in hand
for safety, a barren poem. Ready to bury my face
in abandon, in this balmy California or that.

Vacation Bible School

Little heathens my Gramma must have muttered
under her breath when she helped me and my one
year younger sister unpack, discovering we had
not brought any clothes suitable for church. Strict

Baptists, tucked away in southern Indiana, she felt
we needed instruction after finding out we knew
nothing, learned nothing from our day-long session
at their church. So she combed out her dark brown

helmet hair, stepped into a slip and dress, marched
us across the street to the local schoolhouse and
enrolled us in Vacation Bible School. Dressed
exactly alike with the same bowl haircut, we soon

realized we were blank slates in the big classroom
as our classmates chanted Bible verses while we
squirmed in the back row. At recess, my sister
hissed *follow me to the store and forget about this*

stuff. Timid, afraid of punishment, still I went
after her to the tiny store at the town's crossroads
with a hanging light constantly blinking yellow.
Inside the cool building we purchased hot pink

bubble gum and ice cream sandwiches, which
we ate immediately, completely ruining the big
dinner Gramma had labored over all morning. She
didn't notice my flushed face or my sister's cool

demeanor. The next morning, she watched us cross
the highway, waving good-bye. We ditched every morning.
We never told a soul. Gramma never guessed. Our
drunken mother back home would have been amused.

Our father would have laughed or punished us severely,
hard to say which way, and we kept our silence. So
heathens we remained despite our trusting grandmother
who never ever imagined our transgression.

The Kill Me Pills

—after Anne Sexton

Like her, I regard suicide seriously.
I want the *clickety, click* from the depths
of my purse. She calls them her *kill me pills*
while I call them *my answer*. Anne's

far more dramatic while my plan is plain
as toast. Both of us so practical. At first
I'm an innocent, death always present
through countless therapy sessions,

massive breakdowns, hospitalizations.
I devise a plan, tape a bottle beneath
the dining room table—who would search
there? Chatting with my husband, it falls,

and he heads directly to the bathroom to flush
my safety net away. Gone. Bereft, I need
a new idea. So I cull them slowly, skipping
part of a dose at a time. When I'm in need,

I have them but locked in my bedroom, the
dose isn't enough. I need to worm secret
stashes in the living room down the hall.
But my eighteen-year-old daughter's still

awake and I cannot escape to fish them out
of my grandmother's teapot in the breakfront
or in my purse, primly sitting on the sideboard.
Where are you going, Mom echoes when

I open my door. Early morning and I'm writing
my suicide note. Insomnia for days, I end up
asleep, instead of dead. Those pills confiscated
by my therapist chatting up my daughter via a phone call

that saves my life. But today I'm prepared,
keeping pills always with me, rolling at the bottom
of my leather bag. I collect a couple of kinds
of pills that would do the trick. I'm not strong

enough, brave as Anne who boldly carries her
bottle everywhere, allows people to know her
possible plan. It's time. A simple matter
to pop open the bottle, spill pills into her

elegant palm, wash them down with bourbon
or brandy. She dies smoothly, crystal decanter
falling from her tapering fingers and onto
the floor. I remember her death vividly

as a powerful dream. A shock in my early days
of poetry though even when hearing the news,
I admire her moxie. I don't know when
it will be the correct time to gather

and devour, greedy fistfuls crowding
my gaping mouth. At last, I will be just
like Anne, her voice hard and flat as she enters
the right time, the final time, the end.

Handbag

—after Ruth Fainlight

My mother's heavy summer straw bag,
jammed with scarf and sunglasses, crowded
with objects she loves. Odor
of Camel straights and matchbooks.
Mints unraveling in wrappers.
Red lipstick she will chew from her lips,
in time, softened by flesh as it spreads
from edges into smears. Often
she allows me to carry it. Heavy odor
of *Tigress* cologne, cheap stuff.
Powder puff and compact, the bottle
of gin she drinks from. Her idea of womanliness
and her own anguish I grow to cherish,
dislike, disdain, and never to love.

Discarded Tears

My father sings *good night ladies*
as he lapses into a coma. I begin
to sob. I will not be silenced, until

I'm sedated. I sweep into the funeral
in a black velvet gown, skirt skimming
the floor. A vintage dark-blue crystal brooch
adorns my left breast, right above my heart.
It's nearly the color of my eyes, something

we don't share. Stepfamily/ acquaintances/
church officiants/ seek cover from sparking light,
dazzling rays. How many my discarded tears?
The barbershop group fills six rows of bleachers
while they attempt to harmonize. Pastors speak
silly talk before bologna sandwiches are served.

The night before, he returns, fresh
from an enormous icebox. Leaning into the casket,
I kiss his forehead. Cold as winter, cold as clay. *Good*
I say to myself. *This time he is truly dead, in ruins.*

Sometimes still my father comes to me at night,
wanting to nuzzle a kiss. His hammy hands
tap my body as if I'm forever childhood's
furnace. The young one who says *don't,*
the young one who says *take me now.* How tired
I am of speaking dreams where I'm too little
to understand—he bleeds me into plummy clouds,
I grow at my father's boot-shod feet.

After Midnight at the Psych Hospital

Come see the moon, Wendy says softly,
sticking her head inside my room's door.
I've been resting since dinner, not a single
positive thought in my head. *It's cold, but*

worth a trip outside she says and staggers
away, leaving me behind. Sighing with
exhaustion, I climb off the bed, covered
with my lucky blanket and pillows. I haven't

made much progress in this hospital,
450 miles from home, and I'm discouraged.
I'm still numb to my core. I'm locked
in this closed hospital with twelve women,

all sexual abuse survivors, every one of us
struggling with psych issues. It isn't
a simple place. I follow Wendy down the hall,
past the nurses' station where eight women

camp out, having dragged their mattresses
by orders from their therapists to be watched
all night by nursing staff so they don't
self-harm. My new roommate's here, wrists

wrapped daily in fresh bandages she rips
with her nails, again and again opening up
the wounds that bring her to this hospital.
For about a week Wendy was my roommate

but her constant screaming from nightmares
woke me, leaving me unable to sleep.
I was tired mornings, unable to participate in
group therapy sessions. I liked her, hated

to move, but I had to find sleep. Still, we're friendly,
share a love of poetry. I trail her out the back door,
the only way outside, where a couple of women
chat. *Look* Wendy says *how lovely it is.* And

above us is a thick yellow moon, with rings
surrounding it. I'm guessing the circles
are mostly pollution from LA. But it seems
to spin, its fat face smiling down on us.

Somehow it seems to say *everything
is going to work out*. It's a promise I need
to see and hear. Maybe it will propel my case
from dysfunction to on-the-road home, just

meds and my therapist necessary to keep me well.
I told you so Wendy says in the same voice, pointing
one large forefinger toward the heavens. She beams
as the moon rotates away from us, our faces

clearly agog. The two of us are left alone
as the moon moves on to more pressing
business, lives, other wretches to inspire,
scattering everything in its wake.

Virginia Chase Sutton's third book of poetry, *Of a Transient Nature*, was published last year by Knut House Press. Her second book, *What Brings You to Del Amo*, won the Samuel French Morse Poetry Prize, and was published by Northeastern / University Press of New England. *Embellishments* was her first book (Chatoyant). Sutton's poems have won the Louis Untermeyer Scholarship at Bread Loaf Writer's Conference and the Allen Ginsberg Poetry Award, and her poems have appeared in *The Paris Review, Ploughshares, Quarterly West, Amethyst Arsenic, Comstock Review,* and *Stoneboat,* among many other magazines, journals, and anthologies.

Six times nominated for the Pushcart Prize, she holds an MA in literature; and an MFA in Poetry from Vermont College of Fine Arts, where she also did a post-graduate semester, and was a writing workshop assistant for two residencies in the Writing for Children's MFA program.

She was formerly a market researcher, journalist, and tenured English professor—where her work in beginning the college's creative writing program earned her the award, *Innovation of the Year*. Sutton has received financial support for her writing with four grants from *Poets & Writers* magazine, from Scottsdale Center for the Arts, the Arizona Commission on the Arts, Phoenix Public libraries, and the Arizona Humanities Council. A fellow at the Vermont Studio Center, and a fellow over ten times at the Ragdale Foundation, she lives in Tempe, Arizona with her husband.

www.ingramcontent.com/pod-product-compliance
Lightning Source LLC
LaVergne TN
LVHW041553070426
835507LV00011B/1066